Table of Contents

VI. Closing Thoughts: Reimagining a Magazine as Digital Media Marches On

I.

Introduction: Disrupting the Media Model for News and Information

Eight Points of Clarity

The media landscape is packed with grand old brands, many fighting to reinvent their identity. Some are chasing bright, shiny objects; new technology tricks abound. Some are trying to mimic a competitor's ideas ("it's working for them, let's make it work for us, too"). Still others are "Cool Chasers," partygoers fawning over the sexy new "voice" of the Web or the *It* designer of the moment.

Everybody wants some cool. Who wouldn't want a little Miles Davis or Keith Richards in their lives? Actually, I think the *Forbes* message is kind of cool. As the world puts more hope and faith in the spunk and nimbleness of entrepreneurial dreamers, *Forbes* is backing them all the way, just as it always has. My colleague, Tom Post, phrased it well: "Start with clarity, come up with cool," he said. "If you don't, you end up with new but incoherent."

Eight points of clarity have driven our efforts to disrupt the media model for news.

1) Embrace The Content Continuum

At the core of social media, everyone is publishing and sharing content to form deeper relationships with people they know or to connect with those they would like to know. For *Forbes*, "everyone" means the three vital voices of the media business: journalists, the audience and marketers.

We give members of each group the opportunity to publish – or certainly to openly participate and co-mingle – in a credible business news environment. The key is transparency. Everyone's role is clearly identified and labeled. To that end, we've supplemented our full-time staff of experienced reporters with a community of carefully selected qualified contributors (freelance journalists, authors, academics, topic experts and business leaders), each building an audience around their name and knowledge.

For readers and users, we've placed their comments into the natural flow of our Web site and magazine. We've enabled marketers to say what's on their minds, too. Our evolving AdVoice platform gives them the same tools as our journalists and contributors to publish content on Forbes.com and the opportunity to do the same in print, in every case always prominently delineated. In the last two years, we've built a brand-building platform for journalists, participatory readers and marketers – all under the *Forbes* umbrella brand and our mission.

2) Recognize the Individual as a Brand: This trend actually began a century ago (William Randolph Hearst loved collecting celebrity journalists, including B.C. Forbes, our founder). In more modern times, national newspapers, broadcast television and cable turned many anchors (Walter Cronkite), reporters (Sam Donaldson) and columnists (Evans and Novak) into star brands. Each depended on a big media organization for distribution, marketing and so much more. The digital era and social media enable knowledgeable content creators to build audiences and followings on their own. Our full-time staffers now publish under their names, as do contributors, who remain independent operators. They all belong to a curated network of branded experts that naturally attracts other qualified writers who want to be part of a group that now totals 1,000.

3) Build a Labor Model for the Times

The economics of the digital era demand new, more efficient staffing models. The key is a scalable structure that enables qualified voices to provide quality content – and lots of it – to meet the demands of voracious business news consumers.

- We've built a hybrid model that includes full-time editors and reporters and nearly 1,000 experienced contributors across our eight key verticals, all of whom increasingly play the role of content creator, producer and programming manager using a new set of tools we're putting in their hands.

- We've focused on partnering with leading edge start-ups – examples include DayLife, Visual Revenue, Narrative Science, Zemanta, Betaworks, Gesture Theory, Social Amp, Automattic, Athletics (a UI and design shop) and many others.

- We've implemented The New Newsroom: a veteran staff of editors, hard-bitten reporters, tech-savvy digital journalists and our distributed workforce of qualified contributors. Without increasing the number of our salaried staff, we've added a producer desk to support our content creators and an audience development team to help market them across the digital world's varied information ecosystems. They use our state-of-the-art publishing tools and data analytics to create, program and distribute high-quality content.

4) Reimagine Products from the Inside Out

We didn't try to remake a Web site – or a magazine, for that matter – all at once. The time it takes to redesign, deploy technology, rethink the workflow, analyze staff requirements, and then put it all together will make a product outdated immediately upon completion – that is, if the weight of it all doesn't come crashing down on you first (did I ever learn that during eight years at AOL). So, we found our strategic center and built out from there, one code release after another, one magazine template after another.

In a multi-platform, multi-device world, our goal is a fluid branded *Forbes* experience with consistent and continuous engagement across all our products. The starting point was our signature list, *The Forbes 400*. We built a scalable Web profile page that worked for each individual Rich List-er, combining real-time content, data and social connections (we later re-fashioned the page for companies, places, colleges and sports teams). The look and feel and functionality moved easily to the iPad. Simultaneously, we built a compatible multi-layered module-and-template system for *Forbes 400* profiles in print.

5) Make Publishing and Programming Fast and Easy

The new economics of digital media necessitate the blurring of traditional roles and their functions. Today's content creators must be writers, editors, producers and both photo and video editors, often performing all those tasks for one piece of content. That requires easy publishing tools for Web, tablet and mobile production. The trick to that: don't build from scratch, but customize and streamline open source tools for the workflow.

We built tools that give journalists more creative freedom to program, curate and filter content on their pages, lessening the role of content algorithms. We found that site editors needed flexible tools, too. We gave them the ability to mix and match content types (posts, photos, videos, comments, tweets, etc.) and to create experiences that engage consumers with variety and depth.

6) Evangelize a Data Culture: In August 2010, we introduced Web screens with a public page-view counter Suddenly, everyone could see how many times a story had been viewed – the audience, all our authors, their colleagues and their friends. At first, staffers and contributors were uncomfortable. It was upsetting for them to see when their posts didn't attract attention. Many lobbied for the counters to be removed. I've felt for quite awhile that real-time feedback would help journalists better serve their readers. "The data is to inform your journalism, not to rule it," I would say. Then something fascinating began to occur: when the counter wasn't working, publishing slowed to a trickle. The data feedback loop had become that important to our content creators. Today, the counter is working beautifully. Our staffers and contributors are building even bigger audiences. Each has an individualized real-time data dashboard.

7) Join and Engage the Community

The job of a journalist has changed. It's no longer solely about reporting and writing or doing a video stand-up. The entrepreneurial journalist seeks out an audience, then understands it and engages with it. I call it "transactional" journalism. Today's journalist needs to be part of the conversation in such a way that builds loyalty to their individual brand and knowledge. Journalists must work to encourage others to participate in the dialogue and share their content with others.

When staffers, contributors or AdVoice marketing partners publish with our tools, they can choose to simultaneously post their content to Facebook and Twitter (effectively marketing it). Their tweets can similarly be published on relevant Forbes.com channels.

Most important, content creators can manage their communities through our commenting tool. Each staffer and contributor can approve, or "Call Out," user comments that further the conversation in productive ways. Their own comments on each others' pages are automatically Called Out. Only Called Out comments appear on page load. All comments and the entire threaded conversation can be accessed by clicking the "All Comments" tab. The result is a rewarding discussion without the noise. I just love it when someone says to me, "The conversation on *Forbes* is so civil." Our comment system is the reason why.

To me, this feature reflects our emphasis on the authenticity of our digital content. Sure, self-publishing is not always perfect. There are typos, misspellings and sentence fragments that we always do our best to correct quickly through close monitoring. But the information, tied to deep knowledge, context and passion, is what makes the posts and the conversation come alive. Updating, clarification and even correcting should be celebrated as a part of the story process itself. And it should be seen as the ultimate form of audience engagement. It's great to see staffers and contributors engage in intense dialogue with the Forbes.com audience (check out a few such examples here and here).

8) Focus on The Message

For us, there is no better place to showcase our mission than on the cover of *Forbes* magazine. In the issues following our print re-architecture and redesign (which coincided with our site re-architecture, the release of iPad apps and later an upgraded mobile site), we have presented a strong, clear and consistent message: social media is about the individual. Our covers anoint individuals with impact: from Warren Buffett and Jay-Z, to Bernard Arnault, Bill Gates, Julian Assange, Arianna Huffington, Sean Parker, Sheldon Adelson, Clayton Christensen and so many others. We have unique access to the world's most powerful players, and each fits with the clarity of the *Forbes* mission. Each has helped us retain focus in developing our other products.

Thinking and Acting Like a Startup

Forbes is disrupting traditional media, changing and growing in profound ways. We produce, present and pay for much of our content differently. We staff, distribute and market it differently. We put data at the core of everything we're doing – to inform our journalism, not rule it. We listen. We engage. We digest it all. We learn. Then, we adapt and move forward. Digital media is organic, so we work hard to move through it in a methodical manner.

We're approaching the journalistic world with an inquisitive eye and a startup mentality while remaining deeply committed to our traditional media values and standards. We've fast become a platform for content creators across The Content Continuum. When you keep adding talent who otherwise wouldn't being working for you to a growing network of passionate readers, who knows where it can go.

To sum it up: disruption brings joys and challenges. It's very rewarding to produce quality content that attracts a growing audience – and to do so efficiently. Technological innovation can be frustrating when you're serving 1,000 content creators around the world and millions of participatory readers. It's all part of navigating the intersection of the news business and the exploding world of social media. I've never paid more attention to all the feedback, both positive and negative. Never have I had the opportunity as I do now to monitor the analytics of every side of the news business in five-second intervals. Never have I been better prepared to do what I do.

II.

The Forbes Approach to Brand Building

Inspired Beginnings

Forbes is the Bible of success, capitalistic endeavors and wealth, in America and throughout the world. Malcolm Forbes himself jump-started *The Forbes 400* nearly 30 years ago. At first, his editors resisted. They didn't see the "journalism" in it. Today, *The Forbes 400*, or "The Rich List," as it's known in-house, is the single most popular measure of "making it big" for immigrants like Malcolm's father, Russian businessmen, Hip-Hop stars . . . well, for just about everyone, including an entire new generation of college graduates and dropouts hoping to be the next Mark Zuckerberg.

Forbes' legendary editor, Jim Michaels, brought his own special brand of journalism to the magazine and its mission. For more than 30 years, he cut to the heart of what it meant to be a successful capitalist – and often through the hearts of many renowned corporate executives who didn't get it. He lived and breathed the principles of blogging – authenticity and voice – decades before it came into being.

Then, in 1996, with the strong support of Tim Forbes, the company launched a Web site at a time when nearly all major media companies couldn't decide what to do about this thing called the Internet. Many still haven't figured out, but Forbes.com quickly grew to 18 million monthly unique users. *Forbes* took another bold step by deciding to move beyond a Web site to a far more inclusive and scalable publishing platform. Knowing the world demands still more from its media industry, Forbes.com is now a place that puts news – and what I like to call "Entrepreneurial Journalism" – at the center of a social media experience.

The New Forbes Model: Quality, Quantity and Variety

Entrepreneurial Journalism means digital screens that come alive with individual voice, real-time activity and dynamic content, not the homogenized, lifeless and static news pages I see on so many other news sites. When I spoke with *Forbes* staff reporter Deborah Jacobs about this change, she replied, "You know what's changed for me at *Forbes*? I now write for my audience, not my editor."

That's what our new model is about – listening and engaging with news consumers. Then we trust our full-time reporters and knowledgeable contributors to respond by producing content that meets their needs. And lots of it! Digital audiences can't seem to get enough information, so it's our job to supply it. Our unique model enabled us to provide them with quality, quantity and variety across eight key verticals, or subject areas. Our individually branded content creators, not burdened by outdated bureaucratic journalistic layers, use the publishing tools we built for them to turn out thousands of posts – nearly 100,000 in 2011. It was all about putting business topics (like this post on Best Buy) and cultural events (like this one on Snooki) through the *Forbes* prism of free enterprise, entrepreneurial capitalism and smart investing.

Entrepreneurial journalism also means providing our staffers and contributors with tools that enable them to easily publish text, photos, and video – then knowing they will engage, one-on-one, with readers as passionate as they are about the world of business. It means:

- Putting real-time usage data in the hands of journalists and writers so they can better understand audience interests and consumption patterns.

- Respecting the audience by deeply integrating comments into the flow of our product experiences, online or in print.

- Understanding that our marketing partners are experts, too, and providing them with the opportunity to participate in the news stream.

- Integrating these actions and sensibilities across our print and digital products to create a fluid *Forbes* experience for our three vital constituencies – content creators, the audience and marketers.

The quality, quantity and variety of our content that springs from this type of journalism continues to result in record audiences for Forbes.com. According to a widely used industry measuring service, 30 million unique users now visit our site monthly – through desktop computers, mobile devices and tablets. The huge success and widespread media coverage of our 2012 Billionaires List helped lead us to six consecutive months of record traffic.

This new content-creation model was just the first step in our plans to open up our digital and print platforms to content creators, consumers and marketers alike.

Management Teams for a New Newsroom

We wanted to build management systems for a new era of journalism, not stop-gap solutions for outdated structures based on restrictive editing layers. We worked hard to evolve and improve an organizational construct with new and different kinds of jobs, responsibilities and workflows. It's a system that has enabled us to manage our model for distributed authorship – and to inject as much quality and variety as possible into our quantity.

We are a 95-year-old startup that has built the digital and people structures for the new era of social media. Here's a look at the organization that has helped us attract and support 1,000 content creators and 30 million news enthusiasts.

Staffers: We have at the core of our organization an experienced and passionate group of full-time editors and reporters. For the magazine, our editors continue working pretty much as they always have. For our digital operations, they act more like product managers, working with our sales, technology and marketing teams. They are particularly focused on what I like to call "editing talent" – that is, carefully screening and selecting the topic experts for our contributor base.

Contributors: As our staffers report both daily and in-depth stories, the authors, academics, topic experts and business leaders who make up our contributor base provide our audience with context, perspective and analysis on the day's events (many do their own reporting, too). A significant percentage of contributors are part of an incentive-payment program based on the loyal audience they attract (right now, 25% of my budget for pure content creation is allotted to contributors). Others find reward in association with our brand.

Producers: They are a key component of The New Newsroom, supporting our content creators in every way and helping to maintain and improve quality. They are masters of our powerful new publishing tools.

Audience Development: Another key player in The New Newsroom, AD, as we call it, focuses on Search Engine Optimization, Social Media Optimization and building distribution partnerships. Working with our editors, content creators, and producers, they helped lead the way to a seven-fold increase in our traffic from the top five social sites.

Product Team: These are the folks who drive our consumer experiences across desktop, mobile, tablet and video. They envision, then execute on product design, user experience, our publishing tools and much more.

Technology Development: This was the team that built it all, from our tools, to our pages, to our statistics engine, to everything else. They put their heads down and got it done, one code release after another.

Partners: We believe in building on the backs of giants: WordPress, Google, Facebook, YouTube and others. We also love working with startups – Betaworks, Narrative Science, Visual Revenue – and the design and user experience collective, Athletics, which has been so core to our suite of digital products.

Evolving Forbes and Extending the Brand

Our magazine's people-centric cover strategy has been in total sync with the world's growing focus on the individual as a content creator and change agent. Our digital strategy enabled 1,000 writers to attract, connect and build an audience around their individual brands and expertise. Forbes.com has evolved into a full-fledged publishing platform and a budding social media operating system for business enthusiasts.

You can't stand still in the media business today. Bold experimentation is required. It's clear that our rapidly growing audience enjoys the participatory nature of our platform – and the quality, variety and quantity of what we have to offer. By opening up our platform and building a scalable content-creation engine we have extended the *Forbes* brand to all those who believe in the principles of free enterprise and entrepreneurial capitalism. We are excited by our progress, knowing we need to work even harder to produce authoritative journalism. Our goal is to stay focused, avoiding the chase for bright shiny objects that distract so many in our business.

We recognize and embrace the need for an all-inclusive conversation. Consumers want their voices to be heard on an equal playing field with content creators. Marketers want to get their message across in new ways that enable them to form deeper relationships with the audience, thought leaders and journalists.

The aim at *Forbes* is to spark and facilitate this dialogue with legitimacy and transparency. If we can accomplish that in some small measure, we can help ensure the future of a vibrant free press. In far simpler media times, that's just what B.C. Forbes set out to do.

"Called Out" Comment

diankrose commented:

I appreciate what you're doing at Forbes on so many levels. One is the holistic approach to your content initiative. In so many cases, content change is done haphazardly and without any consideration of the end product or how the pieces work together – a little tweak here, a little tweak there – in an attempt to jump on a digital trend. Clearly, you get it. I also appreciate your commitment to respect content creators, their knowledge and the craft of good writing. Your strategy to "produce great content and strengthen our audience" cannot be accomplished without smart, capable people who also can string together well-written sentences in a logical manner. Thank you for recognizing this oft-overlooked aspect of content creation. My hope is that your model will inspire others who also are trying to figure out how to be successful in today's complex media environment, and make my search for knowledge and my reading experience less painful than it has become in the last few years.

I responded:

Thx so much for your interest. We have a long way to go, and we learn something every day about the "path forward." I am very committed to the journalistic values and standards that we both believe in.

III.

Digital Journalism and the New Face of Media

The Business of Writing – Online

For the longest time, I felt news was a calling. Report the facts. Cultivate your sources. Uncover information. Write the story for the public good. Journalism was – and still largely remains – a top-down, one-to-many business, with the same "voice of God" formula that one TV executive vowed to do away with but never did. I still see it as a calling, though I must admit to some cynicism after 35 plus years doing this. But I've definitely shed my arrogant journalistic upbringing. Today, I believe digital news is like the Web itself – that is, a transactional affair.

The Web is the ultimate marketplace, where goods and services – as well as news, information and ideas – are exchanged. The medium's effectiveness has been pretty clear for commerce, especially with the arrival of Google AdSense. Advertisers feel the potential, too. The Web's impact on the news media is not dissimilar. Sure, traditional news media can stimulate a response, but the response is discontinuous – it requires a separate channel, such as the Postal Service or an 800 number – and it's never permitted to have equal weight. The Web is a channel that both stimulates and fulfills. It's one and the same because its tools help to blur the line between sellers (that includes journalists) and buyers (that includes news consumers).

Now, journalism is not commerce and it's not advertising. But no longer is the journalist addressing the abstract notion of "the reader." On the Web, the author connects one at a time with individual readers, right down to the IP address. That means journalists now must engage, or "transact," accordingly.

Along with the declining influence of the portals and the rise of social media, digital news is now in the hands of everyone, not an elite few. This does not at all negate our (mine, too) rich heritage. In fact, the demand for what we do is stronger than ever. Journalists simply need to get in tune with their audience, which is really what our business is all about, and we need to draw on our heritage to effectively practice transactional journalism.

This all became much clearer to me after we released a new Forbes article page in August 2011 – a template for authoritative news in this unfolding era of social media. It was further reinforced when we added a comment strip under a post's headline to show the avatars of readers whose remarks had been Called Out. Our article page had put the journalist – or the topic-specific expert – at the very center of a community of followers, particularly those the journalist had transacted with.

Lewis DVorkin, Forbes Staff
I fixate on the intersection of digital journalism and social media.
+ Follow on Forbes (383) ✓ Subscribe 12k

BUSINESS   4/30/2012 @ 6:25AM   2,595 views

Inside Forbes: The 9 Realities of Building a Sustainable Model for Journalism

19 comments, 18 called-out   + Comment now

Jason
I agree and disagree with your statements. I agree that there are many sites, journalists, bloggers, etc, etc that do simply incite more hype, propaganda, [...]

decades in the news industry, one of them in new media, to guide me. During my journey, I've kept two quotes locked in my mind. This one, from Don Logan, the former CEO of Time Inc., in response to how much he spent building the ill-fated Pathfinder Web site: "It's given new meaning to me of the scientific term black hole." The other was from Jeff Zucker, NBC Universal's former CEO. In talking about digital video, he said: "Our challenge with all these ventures is to effectively monetize them so that we do not end up trading analog dollars for digital pennies."

The evolution of the newsroom continues. (Credit: Gimme Rewrite, Sweetheart... Tales from the Last Glory Days of Cleveland Newspapers, by John H. Tidyman)

Both were so right. I worked at AOL for eight years (Logan actually took charge for a brief, not-so-shining moment). I witnessed how strategic indecision can flush money down the digital drain.

The Long and Short of Storytelling

When I first transitioned to the digital world more than a decade ago, my traditional media colleagues ribbed me for abandoning "real" reporting in favor of the fast and the short. No one reads in-depth stories online, they said. When I started *True/Slant*, that just confirmed it for them. I had once and for all gone over to the dark side of journalism (never mind that our top contributor at *T/S* consistently wrote 2,000-word posts).

Perhaps audiences back then did gravitate to shorter fare. But today, they want it all. Some readers want short-form content, others long-form and still others the short-form version of the long-form. Journalists need to meet all consumer needs. As we build out our strategy at *Forbes*, veteran journalists – like Eric Savitz, our highly respected Silicon Valley Bureau Chief, and Matt Herper, one of the nation's top pharmaceutical writers – and the digital-savvy reporters of a new generation are using our highly customized publishing, commenting and data tools to discover and serve audiences. It's all good for journalism, and for building the new media experiences required by today's audiences, which are as fragmented as the media itself.

The fact is, long-form and short-form can work hand in hand. In the case of our magazine cover on billionaire Sheldon Adelson and his vast casino, hotel and resort business, we paired the cover article with a sidebar on his $11 million investment in Newt Gingrich's presidential ambitions. Published on Forbes.com on a Tuesday, the sidebar was intended partly to generate interest in the longer cover story, which we posted the following day. Both were heavily shared across the social Web, particularly on Facebook.

But we're not the only ones finding success with long-form content in the digital era. In an email exchange I had with Mark Amstrong, the founder of Longreads.com, Mark attributed the "resurgence" of long-form journalism to a number of factors:

1. The embrace of mobile devices and tablets.

2. The rise of social recommendation – when people read something they really love, they become its biggest cheerleader.

3. A community that has embraced a new way to organize this content (#longreads).

4. The rise of time-shifting apps like ReadItLater [Mark is an adviser there]. The ability to take a story offline with you – and finish it in places where you might not have wifi – is critical to the success of long-form content.

Mark pointed me to a post by ReadItLater, which enables consumers to save content from their browser or more than 300 apps and read it later on most devices – with or without an internet connection. Perhaps not surprisingly, the data from more than 100 million articles on ReadItLater shows that consumers save articles consistently throughout the day. But here's when they're reading it:

- Computers: 6pm-9pm
- iPhones: 6am, 9am, 5pm-6pm and 8pm-10pm ("the moments between tasks and locations")
- iPads: predominantly 8pm-10pm.

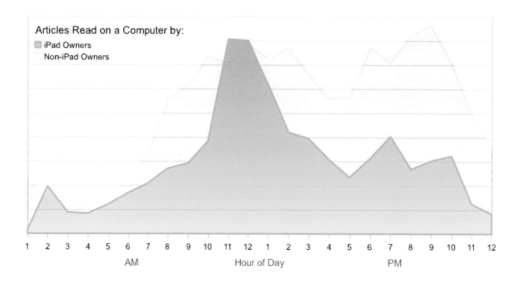

The ReadItLater graph shows both time-shifting and device-shifting for iPad owners reading saved articles.

Longreads, ReadItLater, InstaPaper and other similar ventures are discovery engines for long-form content created by publishers like *Forbes*. There are also startup publishers finding success in original long-form digital content. The Atavist is one. Evan Ratliff, a co-founder, mentioned in an email discussion that The Atavist wanted to create

"a place that first of all allowed us to publish a certain length [5,000-35,000 words] of quality nonfiction story, between magazine articles and books, sold as individual issues. So in our app we lace our stories with integrated audiobooks, maps, timelines, music, animations, video – whatever the particular tale calls for."

In its first year, The Atavist sold more 100,000 copies of 10 titles ($2.99 for multimedia, $1.99 for text), each heavily reported narrative nonfiction. The company hopes to launch a subscription business this year.

The Human Newswire vs. The Medical Marvel

Eric Savitz, our Silicon Valley Bureau Chief, is admiringly referred to within *Forbes* as the "Human Newswire." He's up at 5 am Pacific time, writes 10 posts a day (with market-timed bursts at 6:30 am and 1 pm) and is often spotted posting into the wee hours of the next morning Eastern time. "It's a good approach for a workaholic," he says. Eric zeroes in on the intersection of technology and investing, focusing on the public markets. "My approach reflects the nature of the trading day. I keep my posts short and punchy, and where I can I try to provide a perspective on why things matter in a historical context." Eric squeezes in more expansive digital and magazine reporting when he's not focused on his other responsibilities.

The frequency and timeliness of his posts attracted the news-seeking audience in greater numbers. "When chip companies issue earnings warnings, that has resonance for PC makers, and therefore matters to retailers," he says. Eric was also ahead of the reporting pack in covering the floods in Thailand, as "it was clear to me early on those events would have wide-ranging effects on companies with no direct exposure to the flood waters."

The average number of page views for his popular posts more than doubled, to 10,000, in the second half of 2011, driving his monthly unique visitors sharply higher. His output remained steady, 1,000 posts in the first half of the year and the same in the second half. By continually covering many of the same companies, he built a loyal base of followers (100,000) who visit his page more than once a month. That last statistic would be particularly meaningful for an incentive-based, non-staff digital contributor. The bigger their repeat, or loyal audience (as opposed to once-a-month visitors), the bigger the monthly compensation.

Matt Herper is another among the many talented staff writers and knowledgeable contributors who built audiences around their expertise and individual brands on Forbes.com. Matt's a walking, talking, posting encyclopedia of nearly everything that has to do with medicine. He has a strong following, too.

Matt posts far less frequently than Eric, but in much greater depth. Matt started out posting quite a bit, but reduced his output as he discovered the long-form rhythm worked best for the topic, his audience and his traffic numbers. "I think it's partly because, in medicine, a lot of the challenge isn't just pointing out what is important, but also why," Matt says. "For a piece to be really valuable, you may need to take the reader into another world." His audience trended up even as his output dramatically slowed down. He also works his audience:

"I promote pretty heavily on Twitter, where I try to stay very engaged. I think about Yahoo Finance, and I'm starting to think a lot about LinkedIn, where the point seems to be to get passed around among a group of extremely well-informed, professional readers, which then leads to even more well-informed, professional readers finding my work."

Matt also engages with them. Using our comment moderation and filtering tools, you can always find him mixing it up with audience members who join the conversation. Additionally, Matt was able to rely on outside experts to cover breaking medical news for us. He brought on 10 or so knowledgeable writers. With Matt's "orbit" of talent, he had more freedom to focus on longer stories. As he says, "I don't need to worry about what might have been missed."

Last November, Matt wrote a powerful magazine cover story on the philanthropic efforts of Bill Gates, who is bringing his marketplace mentality to supplying impoverished children around the world with much-needed vaccines. The story generated a big audience when first published on Forbes.com. When traffic began to wane, Matt did something shrewd. He published a lengthy related post from material that never made it into the magazine cover package – the stuff that fell on the cutting-room floor. That post generated strong traffic, too. Matt also used those pages to promote his original cover story and the Herper brand.

There is really something much bigger at work in all this. Content is content, long-form or short-form (our reporters have succeeded with both strategies). And content is not really print or digital. Media organizations – both new and traditional – place it where they do solely for business reasons. A new breed of voracious news consumer will simply discover it, consume it, talk about it, share it – and even create new content around it – whenever they want on the platform and device of their choice.

"Called Out" Comment

Jon Tesser added his comments about a response from fellow commenter Abraham Hyatt:

Abraham's comment is accurate. I've noticed at our publication that we lose a large majority of users on the first page (and thus bounce rates tend to be high) for long form articles. We're able to draw them in initially through tons of high-powered links, but most users won't stick around for the whole thing. So while it may be true that the heat map is telling you that the "next page" link is the most popular clicked link on the page, I would pay closer attention to the number of users that land on the page and subsequently leave without viewing any other content (otherwise known as bounce rate).

I responded:

Thanks for your comment. I'm well aware of bounce rates, which help track engagement across the site – and I watch those numbers very carefully, too. The topic of this post is pure engagement in the actual longer-form story itself and not our site as a whole. Not only do I use a heat map to measure story-specific engagement, but also another real-time tool from Betaworks that shows me concurrent users on all our pages. Now, if you want to discuss sitewide engagement, that is important, too, and it's changing rapidly in a social media world that is increasingly driven by mobile usage. It's a subject I plan to address in the future.

IV.

News & Social Media - Online Content in the Facebook Age

"The Mullet Strategy": Letting Audiences In

Arthur Miller, the American playwright and one-time college reporter and night editor, said a good newspaper was like "a nation talking to itself." Back then, it was editors and reporters who had all the say. Many decades later, the media is finally letting the audience join in, too.

The Huffington Post coined a far less elegant phrase, "the mullet strategy," to describe its new, more inclusive conversation. It stood for "business in the front," or a homepage run by editors, and "a party in the back," all the other Web pages ruled by tens of thousands of raucous commenters sounding off about one thing or another.

The conversation has been and always will be at the heart of the media industry. As technology amplifies today's strident and disparate voices, many of us in digital media are working to keep the talk productive – or at the very least civil.

I can certainly speak to the challenges of online commenting: I once ran AOL News and Sports. We were late to open our nearly 1 billion monthly pages to commenting, but once we did it got ugly fast. There was no topic that didn't end up in the gutter. After helping to launch TMZ.com, I encouraged its editors to permit commenting. Saying a celebrity had a "puffy face" (remember the Ashley Judd brouhaha?) would have been tossed aside as boring in that comment cesspool.

The love 'em/hate 'em reality of user comments periodically finds center stage. Many Web sites try to thwart shouting and abusiveness by deploying technology filters. That can work, but the real solution is personal accountability. At *Forbes*, it's the core of our digital self-publishing platform: each staffer and contributor is responsible for getting their journalism right. (I never quite understood why a lower-paid fact checker was responsible for making sure a higher-paid reporter's quotes were accurate). They also must take responsibility for their communities, and set the tone of the conversation.

Forbes has a moderated commenting system. Writers need to "Call Out" productive user commentary – defined as remarks that add information, reveal personal experience, or offer interesting perspective and provocative analysis. Useless comments in a thread, or highly repetitive or shrill arguments, should *not* be Called Out, but can be accessed by clicking an "All Comments" button. If readers want the noise, well, it's all there for them to drown in. Our job is to filter, not censor.

There will likely never be a perfect comment system. Recent conversations like this one in our leadership channel, this on gaming and this on Kobe beef sales practices gave me great confidence that ours is headed in the right direction. In each discussion, you'll notice one of our staffers or contributors played a central role by responding to the audience or highlighting comments in a timely fashion. I'm often asked why the conversation on Forbes.com is so interesting. A comment system that rewards thoughtfulness, not volume, is the answer.

The conversation on Forbes.com is growing. Since enabling consumers visiting Forbes.com to use their IDs and passwords from Facebook, Twitter, LinkedIn, Google + and other social accounts to sign up and comment, our registrations and comments have doubled. For these reasons and more, we've talked about giving commenters certain privileges based on what we call "desired behaviors."

The Job of the Journalist is Changing

The unfolding era of social media has transformed the definition, the role – and most importantly, the skills and tasks – of being a journalist. While the news industry is stuck in debate (or fear) over what to do about these realities, *Forbes* is building new models and opportunities for the future.

As they've always done, our staff reporters covering a story for the magazine or Forbes.com call those individuals involved to get facts and quotes. They still ferret out sources to uncover what others don't want them to know. They still write their stories looking through the *Forbes* prism of entrepreneurial capitalism, adding context based on their breadth of business knowledge. Our contributors, all hand-picked by our editors and reporters for their knowledge, perform similar tasks. They share with their digital audiences the information they'd gathered or already possess from long careers in their chosen profession.

Increasingly, our reporters and contributors have become all-purpose, multi-dimensional digital producers, publishing all forms of content on their individually branded Web pages.

Here's how they did it.

- **Tightly focus your angle – and get up early:** Eric Savitz defines his beat very precisely: "I cover the intersection of technology and investing." Eric has a solid following on Facebook, Twitter, and LinkedIn. He uses a Twitter feed to publish an RSS feed on all three services with links to all his posts. And through the *Forbes* partnership with Yahoo, Eric taps the power of Yahoo Finance, making sure to code his posts so they show up on the portal's highly trafficked company pages. "I'm a little obsessive about headlines; I like them snappy, and I make sure they are on point, which helps from an SEO perspective. I make sure to use at least some modest piece of art on every post."

- **Become the go-to industry expert:** There is no more respected reporter on the pharmaceuticals beat then *Forbes* staff member Matt Herper. He's always had a goal:

to write stories that people will remember. "What's changed," he said, "is that the conversation can help people remember and lead to even better stories." To become the known expert that he is, Matt said he talks to as many people as possible, then synthesizes what he heard. "That syntheses – not the drumbeat of news – is what I think my audience really wants." Matt's also active on Twitter, connecting with everyone from former Pfizer research chief John LaMattina (@John_LaMattina) to critics of antipsychotic drugs like @WriteWithStan and @soulflsepulcher.

- **Work the digital community:** *Forbes* staffer Kashmir Hill covers the privacy beat – with a twist. Most journalists covering privacy tend to be "privacy maximalists," Kashmir said. "I started with the premise that our privacy IS eroding in the digital age – and how it's not always as bad as the maximalists make it seem." By inserting her own experience into her posts, Kashmir said readers often tell her "they feel like I'm navigating the pitfalls of privacy along with them." Kashmir's a pro at digital networking. Breaking a big story or two online also helped: Supreme Court Justices rarely speak to the media, but she got Justice Antonin Scalia to comment after a law professor compiled a digital dossier on him.

- **Collaboration leads to community:** Contributor Michael Humphrey identified his angle and went right after the players. His plan was to analyze a new breed of "Technotainers" – what makes them popular, what traditional entertainers can learn from them, or even why they should worry about them. Michael is effectively aggregating his audience by appealing to the audiences of the entertainers through his posts. "The more I dig into a particular platform (YouTube, for instance), the more my own blog becomes a destination. It grows from profiles to trend writing." Michael was able to "attract readers, gather grassroots information" about growing trends and establish himself as a trusted resource for how technology is changing the way we entertain ourselves.

For the *Forbes* journalist, the era of social media means engagement far beyond the act of putting together the story. It's also about building community – a loyal audience – that consumes and shares content with others. It's an audience our content creators need to respond to, to take into account, and form a relationship with. Our New Newsroom helps with all that, but many of our content creators just do it themselves.

Techonomy

As it all changes, some things do stay the same. One of those things is *Forbes'* focus on the intersection of technology and entrepreneurial capitalism. In the early 90's, *Forbes* started *ASAP*, a magazine about the digital economy. As others watched and waited, it launched Forbes.com, now a leading business news Web site. A few years ago, it backed my startup, *True/Slant*, a new kind of digital news company. And now it's invested in Techonomy, a fast-starting media and conference business that's all about the innovative and disruptive technology forces that *Forbes* chronicles and champions.

David Kirkpatrick is *Techonomy's* founder and CEO. David's first career was at *Fortune* magazine, where he distinguished himself as one of the media industry's leading technology writers. He was also the creator and host of *Fortune's* annual Brainstorm conference. Following all that, he literally wrote the book on Facebook, calling it *The Facebook Effect*.

Techonomy's first conference in Lake Tahoe attracted the likes of Bill Gates, Eric Schmidt, Reid Hoffman, and others throughout industry, government, and media. "People now have these extraordinary tools of mobile and social change in their hands," said David, "which are giving them this tremendous new empowerment." We all saw the dramatic impact that's had on foreign governments. David saw industry coming face-to-face with the social power of employees and customers and wrote about just that in his provocative, much-talked about *Forbes* cover story, Social Power and the Coming Corporate Revolution.

Looking back at all the magazine pieces, newspaper articles, blog posts, tweets and videos that I've consumed and shared about the media business in the last ten years, I can remember a few others that stopped me in my tracks.

First came EPIC 2014, an eight minute flash movie released in 2004 for presentation at a fictional Museum of Media History. It took the breath away from many of traditional media's elite editors. It captures a world in which the power unleashed by the merger of Google and Amazon reduces *The New York Times* to a "print newsletter for the elite and the elderly." Upon watching it again for the first time in years, the overarching message and the predicted fate of many newspapers still rings true, though the antagonists in the corporate contraction might be very different today.

A few years later came this article, from Michael Hirschorn in *The Atlantic*:

> Not only do you allow your reporters to blog; you make them the hubs of their own social networks, the maestros of their own wikis, the masters of their own many-to-many realms... Go even further: incentivize the [pop-culture] critics and reporters by allowing them to profit based on the popularity of their sites; make it worth their while to stick around.
>
> – via Get Me Rewrite!, December 2006

Hirschorn's thoughts on how to "save" the newspaper industry made me spring from my desk chair at home on Thanksgiving day, run down the stairs to find my wife and tell her that someone had stolen my idea. Of course, the author hadn't, and I later told him that story. His idea was similar to one I was working on that eventually resulted in *True/Slant*, the startup I founded. Now, with much updated thinking, it's a lot of what we're up to at Forbes as we incentivize experienced and knowledgeable content creators to build audiences around their own individually branded pages on Forbes.com. Somewhat eerily, our model loosely matches EPIC's predictions about what would be.

Then came this, from Andrew Sullivan, also in *The Atlantic*:

> Reading at a monitor, at a desk, or on an iPhone provokes a querulous, impatient, distracted attitude, a demand for instant, usable information, that is simply not conducive to opening a novel or a favorite magazine on the couch. Reading on paper evokes a more relaxed and meditative response. The message dictates the medium. And each medium has its place – as long as one is not mistaken for the other.
>
> – via Why I Blog, November 2008

As I was about to head to *Forbes*, I thought a lot about how Sullivan, a great blogger and a great writer, was able to glide from digital to print, making sure his voice was heard and his audience could find him. His personal strategy remains at the forefront of my mind today as we re-imagine Forbes magazine. We're making it possible for staffers and contributors alike to produce content for the chaotic forum of a digital environment, then settle into the "meditative" pages of our magazine by recasting their work from Forbes.com (or just coming up with new stories) for a group of print readers with different needs.

And more recently this, from Paul Ford in *New York Magazine*:

Social media has no understanding of anything aside from the connections between individuals and the ceaseless flow of time: No beginnings, and no endings. These disparate threads of human existence alternately fascinate and horrify that part of the media world that grew up on topic sentences and strong conclusions. This world of old media is like a giant steampunk machine that organizes time into stories. I call it the Epiphanator, and it has always known the value of a meaningful conclusion.

– via Facebook and the Epiphanator: An End to Endings?, 2011

Obsessed with Facebook or not, It makes you think about how journalism is in danger of being reduced to soulless, disjointed nuggets as blogging platforms – and reporting, too – give way to not only Facebook, but 140-character Tweets and text messaging. The arrival of Google+ does nothing to alleviate such a fear. Actually, as it relates *Forbes*, I'm a bit comforted by the notion of The Epiphanator. First, we have a magazine for journalists to momentarily stop the stream so they can reflect and provide that "conclusion" before the reader reaches the "■" (that's how Ford symbolized it) at the end of an article. Second, our digital platform is all about giving topic-specific experts the tools to add context, analysis and perspective before audiences reach a post's "■."

Forbes built a new model for journalism that offers opportunities for knowledgeable content creators to ride the news stream or stop the "ceaseless flow of time." Andy Greenberg stopped it with an exclusive magazine article just as Julian Assange was making headlines every minute. David Whelan did, too, when he told the dramatic tale of Harvard's Clayton Christensen, whose academic research into the medical establishment collided head-on with his personal health issues.

"Called Out" Comment

rlbaty commented:

I'm one! One of the folks who comments on *Forbes*. I'm what might be called an Internet creation; just an inconsequential nobody that has developed a considerable Internet resume. I managed to tick off a number of people in the old days and was told I should set up my own site; so I did, a YAHOO! discussion list all my own. Not long ago I happened to pick up on the coverage some *Forbes* contributors were giving to the tax-cheatin', horn-playin' Phil Driscoll. I checked in and the rest, they say, is history and history in the making. I now have quite a *Forbes* portfolio, including comments and even a guest column. I appreciate the patronage I have received from my *Forbes* sponsor. I would have liked to have generated more and more diverse participation, but maybe it will come.

V.

A New Breed of Journalist - What Makes Forbes Writers Different

Joy's Law & Disruptive Journalism

Have you ever heard of Joy's Law? I had completely forgotten about it until Rich Karlgaard, the publisher of *Forbes*, jolted my memory. It's named after Bill Joy, the co-founder of Sun Microsystems. He came up with one of those ah-ha principles that either impart science or wisdom. Here's what Joy said about life in a fully networked world:

"No matter who you are, most of the smartest people work for someone else."

Rich brought it up in the context of our new model for journalism. We offered smart people working for others – journalists, authors, academics and topic experts – the opportunity to build brands on Forbes.com around their name and knowledge. They complemented the smart editors and reporters already working for *Forbes*. "You've aligned *Forbes* to Joy's Law and built a model that taps this big world of talent," Rich said.

For us, it was all about Entrepreneurial Journalism. It's a disruptive model that gained support from content creators, full-time staffers who built their own brands, digital news consumers, and marketers (more than a dozen have published content on our site or in the magazine).

I asked six *Forbes* contributors to share their experience about being an Entrepreneurial Journalist. Here's what they had to say:

Erik Kain

His angle: "The nerd culture in the age of social media."

Bio: Editor-in-Chief, The League of Ordinary Gentleman; freelance writer for The Atlantic and others.

"Forbes has allowed me to find success that I don't think I ever would have found in the old model of journalism. Besides, I love to write... and will drive as much traffic as possible while still remaining honest and sincere in everything I write. This has been a really game-changing opportunity for me."

Chunka Mui

His angle: "I help companies design and stress-test their innovation strategies."

Bio: Managing Director, Devil's Advocate Group; Co-author, *Unleashing the Killer App: Digital Strategies for Market Dominance* and *Billion-Dollar Lessons*."

"Consulting engagements last for months and books take years. Given the unrelenting market turmoil and technological disruption, every day's headlines are brimming with inspirational successes and educational failures. Forbes allows me to work on a shorter clock cycle. My aim is to help readers see the non-intuitive angles, separate the hype from the reality, and draw lessons applicable to their own challenges."

"Forbes is helping to define the future of journalism. Forbes.com demonstrates that blogging doesn't replace journalism; blogging enhances journalism. Our challenge will be to deliver greater value, not just more page views. That will require continuing to build the community and enrich the conversation. Gresham's Law is hard to beat."

Nadia Arumugam

Her angle: "I cover food and drink from industry news to current trends."

Bio: Former editor of Fresh, a leading UK food magazine; Contributing Editor, Fine Cooking; Freelance writer for Epicurious, TheAtlantic.com, Saveur and Slate; Her Blog, spadespatula.com; Author, *Chop, Sizzle & Stir*.

"Maintaining ownership of your material entails that there's more onus on the writer to self-edit and make sure that his/her work maintains a certain standard of editorial integrity, which I really appreciate."

"Forbes.com has enabled me to broaden my appeal beyond the niche food audience. It's also provided me with access to sources. What I think I value most is the credibility it offers me. I can rely on it to be an arena where good writing and intelligent and thought-provoking content defines you as a writer, not the ability to post a photo of last night's dinner!"

Ken Rapoza

His angle: "Anything that moves in Brazil, Russia, India and China."

Bio: Lived in Brazil, covered all aspects of the markets for The Wall Street Journal/Dow Jones.

"It keeps me in journalism working for a major, well-read brand. I average over

240,000 visitors a month. I probably have more people reading me here than I did at Dow Jones and the Journal. So those eyeballs have been important in a business that is all about networking, branding and name recognition. It allows me to make okay money working part time. I enjoy the big traffic numbers, competing with colleagues in my beat and outside of it, and seeing my articles on the home page of Forbes.com. I don't work in the office, but I consider Forbes staffers my colleagues."

Posting vs. Writing?

Posting content for participatory consumers is much different than writing for traditional readers. That's just as true for a large site like Forbes.com as it was for our small startup four years ago. At *Forbes*, reporters and contributors need to write for their audience, not their editors. They also need to "transact" with their readers, that is engage with them one-on-one. It's not an easy transition for die hard journalists to make. In fact, it helps explain what *The Wall Street Journal's* Chicago bureau chief said to me during my very first job interview: "We like to hire college graduates. We don't have to break them of bad habits."

A year into publishing on our platform, Anthony Kosner is ridding himself of some old beliefs. Anthony was a magazine designer for Time Inc., Conde Nast, McGraw Hill and others, then moved into content strategy and Web development. Anthony and I go way back. He was the art director of a magazine I co-founded in the early 90s (I can still remember the 3 am closes and Chinese food), and we've worked on other projects since. He now lives in Portland, Maine. When I first started T/S, he was quite candid with me: "I really don't get where all this is going." Anthony's a smart, inquisitive guy with a deep lineage in the media business, so his skepticism did give me some pause.

Today, Anthony is a believer in our evolving model for incentive-based, entrepreneurial journalism. He uses words like "machine" and "addictive" to describe our publishing platform. In an email exchange after our video interview, he said: "What is so gratifying about the *Forbes* platform is that it rewards the quality of your content. Quantity, timing, relevance and engagement with social media help to make the most of that quality, and in some ways constitute that quality. But it's much more than a numbers game. On *Forbes* you don't have to shout or canoodle to get heard. You just have to write great headlines that are supported by great stories that are about subjects that people actually care about."

Our contributors, all hand-picked by our editors, need to have angles, or beats, that fall within one of our key topic channels. It's largely their responsibility to attract and build an audience and engage with their community, or followers. I love to talk with contributors to see how they're doing. Many are getting it, some remain a bit frustrated. Few have given up. Anthony writes about Web and app developers and the new products they bring to market. To be honest, I find it a little unfocused at times, but he's certainly building an audience. Last month, he had more 400,000 unique visitors, up from the 40,000 he was struggling to maintain early on.

What clicked for Anthony? "At the highest level, I think I was bitten with the challenge and made a commitment to myself to do more and better. So that made me really look at which posts were getting the most attention and try to understand what had legs and why." Anthony says that meant figuring out the intersection points of two dynamics: the news cycle and waves of social media.

Native digital journalists seem to instinctively get those connections. That's not the case for many traditional reporters. If they do figure it out, there's another hurdle to clear: self-promotion. In their mind, that's a dirty job for PR people, not journalists. "You told me years ago," Anthony said, "that this was all about personal branding, about becoming a content brand. I have always mistrusted outward attempts at branding. But I do realize how important it is to support the things you make with appropriately targeted marketing. Otherwise, what you are doing doesn't really exist in any meaningful social way."

As a group, many contributors are finding great success on the *Forbes* platform. Since last June, 55 writers who had already attracted 20,000 monthly unique visitors or more went on to at least double their audience, to as high as 600,000. Many did so, like Anthony, in a matter of months. A handful now periodically break the 1 million monthly reader mark.

Don't get me wrong. Classic reporting skills are desperately needed as journalism moves into the digital age. As I've written here and here, good, old-fashioned fact-gathering, clear and strong writing and topic knowledge is vitally important to *Forbes* as we go about the business of combining our traditional media values with the dynamics of digital publishing. We've had our successes and our miscues. In building The New Newsroom, we continue to get better at educating staffers and contributors alike. We hold regular Webinars on headline writing, the law, social media, basic technology and entering the news cycle. It's not uncommon for 70 to 100 people to participate in each session.

Many journalists are at a crossroads in their professional lives. The media's woes have resulted in layoffs, furloughs and general newsroom belt tightening. Digital publishing and social media have unleashed far more competitive voices than traditional news organizations are accustomed to. Anthony, like others, has found a home on Forbes.com. "For the past few years," he said, "I have been researching what's been happening in a bunch of corners of technology – web development, product design, mobile apps, content strategy, social media – and also several branches of scientific and social research.

Suddenly I realized that at *Forbes*, I had a container for all of that information and an audience that was interested in many of the same things."

I get what Anthony is saying. I've written much more under my own brand on Forbes.com than I ever did at *True/Slant*. For better or worse for my audience, I felt it important to share my nearly 40-year journey through the media landscape. Anthony says writing has increased his skills as a digital designer and developer. My posts have helped me better understand the challenges of moving a traditional media company into the future. It's certainly made it easier for each of us to keep up with the conversation that propels us forward in one new exciting way after another.

Simply put, *Forbes* is about great journalists and all the people out there we can find who know the most about the topics that business news enthusiasts are interested in. It's how we do journalism.

The End of Long-Form Journalism?

The future is bright for all forms of journalism, long-form included. The supply of credible – and I stress credible – information can't seem to meet the insatiable demand for news in the digital era. If you want to cover a beat and write a 5,000-word story, then you need to find and build an audience for it – and that takes time and a new level of expertise. The rise of digital publishing, social media, and the resulting audience fragmentation requires journalists – for that matter, all content creators – to embrace and learn new ways.

I seem to have touched a journalistic raw nerve in discussing in-depth reporting and writing, and how it's finding a digital audience on Forbes.com, ReadItLater, longreads, The Atavist, and other Web sites, apps, communities, and startups that aggregate inquisitive readers. Nearly all the comments expressed some anxiety that a cherished media form was in danger of extinction and a measure of relief that perhaps there was still hope after all.

"Called Out" Comment

Abraham Hyatt posted:

When you note the pageviews that the long-form *Forbes'* posts received, how are you accounting for pagination? The pageviews on the last page of the story, not the first show how many readers are interested in long stories. That's slightly oversimplified; there are a lot of ways that people can view a post as a single page. But as a whole, I think it's more complicated than looking at who hits the front page. Either way, I used to have the same attitude that you did that visitors don't read long stories. Over the last two years it's been a nice surprise to find out how wrong I was.

I responded:

Good points and good question. I can tell you this. I have a 'Heat Map' on all Forbes.com pages that shows me where users click on the screen. I've been stunned that the No. 1 click (it shows me the Top 10) on the first page of nearly all paginated stories is the 'Page 2' link or the 'Next Page' link. And if the post is three pages, way more often than not the No. 1 click on Page two is 'Page 3' or 'Next Page.' I hope that answers your question.

The Tools of the Trade

Forbes, a traditional media company that deeply believes in the values journalists hold dear, is leading the way to new forms of engagement by making it possible for our editors, staffers, and hand-selected contributors to publish on Forbes.com, so their voices can be heard amid all the noise.

It takes work on the contributor's part:

- Using our "Headline Grab" tool to share what they're reading

- Writing short posts, long ones, and everything in between on our highly customized WordPress platform

- Using our tools to drag-and-drop photos into their posts, or inserting photo galleries that they assemble

- Creating videos or embedding relevant videos in their stories

- Inserting charts and graphics

- Programming related content of *their* choice with our Vest Pocket tool (what I consider the bridge connecting our 1,000 knowledgeable staffers and contributors with the 6,000 people and organizations that we track and they often write about)

- "Calling Out" rewarding and productive users comments – and responding to those comments

- Simultaneously publishing on Forbes.com, Twitter and Facebook

- Activating Facebook Subscribe

- Working with our producer desk to master the tools and our Audience Development team to tap the Web's many information ecosystems for readers

As Andrea Spiegel, who runs our digital product development said: "We're building the tools so journalists can determine how best to cover their beat to serve the audience they want to build."

Forbes has become a disruptor in the media industry, but that doesn't mean we can just sit back. Disruptive competitors are everywhere, and journalists need to grasp that concept for themselves. They've been disrupted by a new breed of native digital reporter who grew up with the new tools of the trade, just like I grew up using a CRT rather than an IBM Selectric. And they've been disrupted by all the knowledgeable people out there who can publish content even without working for a newspaper, magazine, broadcast or cable network – and find an audience through social media (no home page traffic required).

So, if journalists learn the tools, study the usage data and engage with their audience through desktop, mobile, tablet, and print, too, then they've got a good shot at a future in long-form, short-form, and every type of journalism in between. There's a big World Wide Web out there. There's Google search. There's this new thing, the Social Web (Facebook, Twitter, and LinkedIn). Focus on your expertise, write great headlines, and engage, I tell them: Go find your audience.

Curation vs. Editing

Aggregation vs. Curation. Journalism vs. "Churnalism." In the first tit-for-tat battle, Bill Keller of *The New York Times* takes on Arianna Huffington of the Huffington Post (or is it AOL?) In the second, it's substance over page views (never mind they're not mutually exclusive). Sarah Lacy and Paul Carr stated:

"Make no mistake there's a battle raging for the soul of new media. Not the clichéd war between print and Web or between Silicon Valley and New York, but rather a series of internal battles being fought within nearly every publication. It's the battle between journalism and churnalism."

– via Journalism vs Churnalism Battle Rages On.

Ah, the "soul" of media. How it reminded me of the 1980's with its now-quaint battle lines. On the one side, *USA Today* (with its snappy graphics and McNugget stories) and *Entertainment Tonight* (remember Mary Hart and the $2 million insurance policy on her shapely legs?). On the other, the "real" journalists, fighting for stories long enough to say something and mighty issues over fleeting celebrity (wonder who won that one?).

I'll weigh in with a little twist: to me, it comes down to Curation vs. Editing. More than aggregation, more than "churnalism," curation was considered in so many ways the next phase of edited journalism. Just as significant, curation-editing was fast transforming "who" the media is.

For nearly 100 years, *Forbes*, along with many traditional publishers, was about editing – words, sentences, paragraphs, stories, voice. We "edited" talent, too, carefully selecting the editors and reporters who wrote the words and filtered the stories that delivered our message and world view. What did all that add up to? You guessed it: curation.

The *Forbes* news experience, like so many others, evolved, but we remained steadfast in our focus on editing, or curation. The thing was, our competitors started to look different. They didn't so much resemble our fellow Big Media companies any more. They increasingly looked like you and me – that is, members of the news audience.

On the Web today, knowledgeable people can publish content for next to nothing. With the tools of social media, those same people can build followings for next to nothing. Both are what *Forbes* and other traditional players do – for significantly more than nothing. Bottom line: there are lots of new, talented editor-curators out there who are attracting an audience using different labor, distribution and economic models.

Forbes adapted to this world while still adhering to what made us a trusted business news provider. We extended the *Forbes* brand to the new world of experienced, topic-specific content creators; to business news consumers who want to "follow" them and engage in conversation; and to marketers, who now publish content as experts both on Forbes.com and in *Forbes* magazine. We called it "the content continuum," and in all cases the content creator was clearly identified and labeled.

Forbes is at the forefront of the new editor-curator world. Yes, we dynamically aggregate content to help round out our digital experience. In fact, we take aggregation a step further. We provide our staff members and contributors with an easy-to-use headline tool that enables them to both curate and aggregate the Web for their audiences. Human curation and human aggregation.

In everything we've done at *Forbes*, I have constantly stressed that we need to give our staffers and contributors the publishing tools to do it all – "from inside the office or on the beach in Tahiti" (that's the mantra of our TechDev team). I want them to be writers, photographers, videographers, curators, and producers of what they do.

Staff writer Dan Fisher (he normally covers finance and the law) did just that with this very real post about falling off the grid during and after Hurricane Irene. Besides explaining his frustrations with losing power, he got the photo, shot the video, and put it all together in a post using our WordPress tools. The New Newsroom curated the remainder of the post experience by inserting two related links (including a photo gallery I created for my Hurricane Post) into the Vest Pocket.

As we moved forward, Dan and his fellow content creators were given additional tools to do what they love to do – create content, dynamically, so their voices can be heard.

Commenters and the New Journalist

I'm a big believer in audience participation. Many news consumers possess knowledge, insights and feedback (comment quality is always more important than volume) that others, journalists included, can benefit from. That type of user information can be just as important as "professional" content – in effect, the equivalent of a post. Fred Wilson, one of New York's most successful venture capitalists and a dedicated blogger, made this observation a few years back and it has remained etched in my brain ever since:

"Here's the thing. I get comments every day on my blog that are as good as any blog posts I see on the Web. And they are stuck behind the comments link. They need to be on the front page, not on the back page."

– via A VC: Comments Can Be Blog Posts.

Of course, there are purely inane remarks, as well as commenters who hijack the conversation. But that's okay. It's the job of Web sites to develop ways to separate the good from the bad.

Many solutions for good versus bad revolve around technology. Some sites enable users to vote up comments. Others deploy language filtering. Still others create tiers of commenters based on desired behaviors or some sort of algorithm. All deploy technology solutions to foster dialogue that can be networked, shared and syndicated.

And then there's comment moderation by living, breathing humans. I have a couple of feelings about this kind of staff moderation. First off, it is expensive and complicated (while at AOL, I dealt with a few community moderation services). Next, it isn't at all clear, at least not to me, what standards are applied to approving or rejecting a comment – or how moderators such as these can make sound editorial judgments across multiple topic areas.

More importantly, it puts the wrong people in charge. The original content creator, that is the journalist, author or whomever, should moderate comments associated with their work. Journalists need to become part of the fabric of their communities. Engaging with audience comments is one great way to do that – your audience will be energized by your participation, no matter how modest it is. There are also ways to "deputize" respected members of your community to help you with the task. The resulting conversation often serves as a new form of story-building, as users provide additional information, relevant links, and even tips for content creators to pursue.

At *Forbes*, we use a customized WordPress commenting system. *Forbes'* full-time staff of editors and writers, as well as our paid and unpaid contributors, have the ability to easily curate and moderate comments on all their post pages. Staff writers and contributors have free reign to respond to their readers, as well as comment on each other's posts. Staff and contributor comments appear automatically, like this one by contributor Rich Unger:

> ### Rich says:
>
> Engaging with commenters is, however, not for the feint of heart. I've spent two days locked in mortal combat because I dared to be a bit critical of Ron Paul! But, as Lewis suggests, that discussion is the point of modern day political and policy writing. If a writer isn't willing to defend the post attracting comment, it is fair to wonder why credibility should attach to that post in the first place.

> ### To which I responded:
>
> Rick, thx for joining this conversation. You do more than defend yourself. You're onstantly explaining, adding information and giving your depth of knowledge on the subject.

The result of these comments is often a multi-faceted, author-reader-contributor conversation that can be more rewarding than the original post. This system enables both content creators and consumers – as participants or observers – to circumvent the noise of commenting.

As we built our content team, we assembled the technology expertise to develop and implement the reporting and editing tools of a new era, not just for our digital journalists, but also for our audience and marketing partners. That way, all those with topic-specific expertise could be part of a dynamic new world of content creation.

This new kind of journalism is continuous and never-ending, because the individual content creator has truly become part of a community. News consumers benefit as full participants in a transparent process that offers more information and context. With all due respect to the talented journalists who came before, it isn't solely about reporting and writing any more. You need to do it all, and be ready to hear from your readers what more there is to do.

"Called Out" Comment

Rich says:

HTML and "the hyperlink" changed everything. With that, suddenly an author ("journalist" or otherwise) can elegantly reference as many other sources and points of view as they care to. So rather than trying to reference some other source or point of view in a rehashed encapsulation (let alone ten or twenty of them), the author can just send the reader directly to the original source, where the source's author can speak for his or herself. What this winds up meaning is that it's never been easier to "cite your source." Of course, there's still a massive need to settle the basic question of "Is this accurate?". This is why good editors and publishers whose reputations are on the line as the promoters of the content will always be highly valuable. With it being so easy to encounter so much content, the value of TRUTH goes up exponentially. Alas, within a given piece, all of the information can be accurate, but still suffer from bias of omission (see also, The New York Times). Whether or not an author chooses to address "all sides" of an issue becomes an question of style, intent, and in many cases, limitations of the reader's time. One might be perfectly able of writing 5000 words on some subject, but knowing that the reader will tune out at 1500 (or 500!), it may be pointless. In the end, with the help of good publishing and content navigation tools, readers will sort it all out, with the best content speaking for itself.

To which I responded:

Dean, Your last paragraph says it all. When content creators and news consumers have access to the same tools, the best content will be found and shared in ways that benefit all.

VI.

Closing Thoughts: Reimagining a Magazine as Digital Media Marches On

Reinventing Forbes

Just ten days into my new job here, Tim Forbes laid a little surprise on me: "Take a look at the magazine," he said. "Now? I replied rather incredulously, already knee-deep into re-thinking Forbes.com." "Yep, now," Tim said with a bit of mischief in his smile.

So I did, and with that my 25 years as a newspaper and magazine editor came rushing back – with one huge difference. I looked at a magazine through the prism of the Web. Design had a new meaning to me. So did stories. So did staffing. So did everything about making a print product.

The simultaneous challenge of radically rebuilding Forbes.com influenced nearly every decision about the magazine – and in ways I would have never imagined. To reimagine *Forbes*, we set our sights on five core areas:

1. Honing our editorial voice
2. Simplifying the magazine's design and flow
3. Reshaping our cover philosophy (no more concept covers, please)
4. Refreshing the model to both create and edit content
5. Thinking through the related digital expressions, particularly for our popular lists

We put a strategic layer above it all: to open up our print platform so readers could participate in more meaningful ways, and marketers could form relationships with both the audience and with thought leaders by producing content themselves that is contextually integrated throughout the magazine.

Many smart people engaged in this effort, including the team at Athletics, a UI and design studio. "So often the media inundates the reader with a mess of visual language that must be digested and deciphered," explained Matt Owens, a senior partner at Athletics. "Our idea for *Forbes* was a visual identity that gets out of the way, that strips away complexity to get to the point."

That's exactly what we set out to do – create a no-nonsense design with a simple architecture for an audience that wants quality content delivered efficiently.

The Content Model: Distributed Authorship & the Voice of Forbes

The evolving and scalable *Forbes* content engine is based on the concept of distributed authorship. In both print and digital, the system helped streamline the editing process and bring the content creator into more direct contact with the business news consumer – and sometimes our marketing partners, too.

Most *Forbes* magazine stories are assigned by editors for use first in the magazine and then published online. Increasingly, Web-first content has found a home in the magazine. When it does, it's always updated and repackaged with additional reporting or print-only elements. One new magazine feature, *The Conversation*, began online as a series of interlinking posts and comments which were subsequently recast for print as a "story" in a conversational format. And soon, marketers who participated in our AdVoice program will have the opportunity to produce content on Forbes.com that will be contextually integrated into *The Conversation* in the magazine.

But before we began to attack all that, and always the first consideration before we embark upon future ventures, we focused on the *Forbes* voice. That was actually the easy part. The *Forbes* mission is so powerful and clear that defining our voice has been far simpler for us than most in the media. Our message remains unchanged after nearly 100 years. We're about free enterprise, the entrepreneurial spirit, investing, success, and the rewards that come with it.

I don't care if you're a weekly, a biweekly, or a monthly, you must offer readers a tightly-focused lens through which to view the world. Your voice must be unwavering, unambiguous, and unapologetic. Magazines that don't put forth an unequivocally clear and authentic voice will be niche-picked to death by more nimble digital brands that will lure readers to their online content.

Clarity like this – for both business news consumers and our staffers and contributors – is more vital than ever.

Design & Structure: Web Teachings

If voice is critical to the success of a magazine, the cover is the megaphone. It announces who you are and where you are taking the reader – both inside the magazine and the journey beyond. The cover fights for attention at the newsstand and the mailbox (I mean the old-fashioned kind, with bills, junk mail and catalogs).

For as long as I can remember, *Forbes* has told its stories through dynamic business leaders, entrepreneurs, and thought leaders. A new approach to collecting and curating content drove the need for a face to match. It was the time to make things clear on the cover by anointing those individuals who are making a difference and changing how we thought.

Then, there's the magazine as it appears beneath the cover. I now looked at a magazine's pacing and flow through a Web developer's eye of consumer navigation and pathing. I spent one career in traditional media (guiding a few redesigns), then another in the digital business (rebuilding AOL's mass-market news, sports and entertainment sites, including TMZ, and then launching *True/Slant*). Those experiences taught me the important differences between design as defined by fonts, photos, and graphics, and design as part of the Web world of modules and templates.

I consistently use both the words re-architect and redesign for a reason: Paint jobs alone don't work anymore (you can no longer spin readers and marketers by relying on design prettiness and that standard old line, "Did you check out our cool new look?"). You need to think through the product and the business imperatives. In a social media world, you need to go beyond the "journalist" as the sole storyteller – and the "story" as processed by editors as the definition of content. Along the way, you must balance the inevitable resource constraints and cost issues associated with repeatedly producing the experience; just because designers want to, and can, doesn't mean you should oblige them. Then you can rebuild the format (that is, the structure) and put a functional design and navigational layer on top of it.

As the system evolved we kept expanding our inventory of modules and templates and we got more proficient at using them throughout the magazine. Always at the top of my mind is the Web sensibility of how users – readers in this case – navigate and path through these elements to consume the product as a whole.

The Art of the Re-Launch

We've accomplished quite a bit at *Forbes*: we launched a new digital publishing platform; we created new people profile pages for the Web; we released new Home page, channel, and section pages. We redesigned a magazine.

My start-up experience as founder and CEO of *True/Slant* taught me a lot. At *Forbes*, I'm learning how to apply that knowledge to re-launching branded products that have already achieved scale. For what it's worth, here are some principles I found to work for me.

- **Stay below the radar screen**. In a Web world, self-promotion creates noise and distraction. Stick with humility.

- **Share the vision**. Internally, spread the direction early and often. Be crystal clear about expectations and success metrics.

- **Be wary of bright, shiny objects and the latest "cool thing."** Keep a tight filter, letting through only those ideas that teach you something.

- **Live the life**: The smartest digital people reside in distant corners. Seek them out, test your ideas, then adjust them. Buy into theirs.

- **Don't send in the clones**. I often say, "You're either in or you're out." But you need bold people who tell you, "You're wrong." And listen.

- **Don't sweat the Org chart**. Set up people with spheres of influence. Break through politics. The structure will form.

- **Brave August humidity in Detroit**. Go visit big customers. You will get push back. It's frustrating, but makes you think harder.

- **Find your** Brooklyn muse. Big Design/UI agencies are the Borg. Find the small shops that know how to balance dreams and dollars.

- **It all happens at the Scrum**. In building products and functionality, the Product and Tech Dev teams must have at it daily. Start at 10:05 am.

- **Check your ego at the database**. In Social Media, you must bow at the sheer complexity of crunching the information. I'd start at 5 am. Daily!

- **Build from Inside Out**. Obsess at the core, work carefully outward. Don't let ideation (hate that word) slow down iteration (love that word).

- **Wait out the journalists**. Some good ones will sadly self-select out the door. So it goes. Early doubters who stay can – and will – surprise you.

- **Real-time data sets you free**. At first, "real" journalists find it crass. Give it time, then watch as great stories evolve and productivity soars.

- **Listen for ringing bells**. You're on to something special when veterans stop to tell you, "I'm really proud to be working here."

- **Go to the gym, watch College Game Day on ESPN**. It clears the mind – and there's lots to learn from the interviews with coaches and players.

Finally, as I like to say, **"All will be well, just get shit done."**

Forbes Forbes, Inc.

Since its founding in 1917, Forbes has been providing insights, information, and inspiration to ensure the success of those who are dedicated to the spirit of free enterprise.

Its flagship publications, Forbes and Forbes Asia, reach a worldwide audience of more than six million readers and its website, Forbes.com—the leading business site on the Web—attracts an audience that averages 30 million people per month. Forbes also publishes ForbesLife magazine and licensed editions in more than 25 countries around the world.

Get more insight. See what the Forbes transformation is about. Get Forbes!

Lewis DVorkin

Lewis DVorkin serves as Chief Product Officer at Forbes Media. His long journey has taken him from The New York Times, Newsweek and The Wall Street Journal, to tabloid TV, AOL—and an instrumental role in launching TMZ.com. DVorkin has lived through a newspaper strike (sounds quaint, right?), the New York City Black Out in '77, and a bout with the Cabbage Patch Dolls. He was the founder and CEO of True/Slant, which Forbes invested in and later acquired.

DVorkin first got hooked on the News business as the student editor of the Daily Iowan during the days of Vietnam, Watergate and Roe v. Wade. He can quote all the best lines from All the President's Men, and still thinks Howard Beale did it better than all the real-life pretenders who followed him. DVorkin would like to express his gratitude to James Bellows—a truly gifted editor, an extraordinary human being and a mentor.

About the Publisher

Hyperink is the easiest way for anyone to publish a beautiful, high-quality book.

We work closely with subject matter experts to create each book. We cover topics ranging from higher education to job recruiting, from Android apps marketing to barefoot running.

If you have interesting knowledge that people are willing to pay for, especially if you've already produced content on the topic, please reach out to us! There's no writing required and it's a unique opportunity to build your own brand and earn royalties.

Hyperink is based in SF and actively hiring people who want to shape publishing's future. Email us if you'd like to meet our team!

Note: If you're reading this book in print or on a device that's not web-enabled, **please email** books@hyperinkpress.com with the title of this book in the subject line. We'll send you a PDF copy, so you can access all of the great content we've included as clickable links.

Get in touch:

CPSIA information can be obtained at www.ICGtesting.com
Printed in the USA
LVIW01n0105090118
562358LV00010B/43